Photographers and in 13 countr have improved th... fantastic photos and artwork using Photoshop Tip Card tutorials.. Now it's your turn!

"Your way of explaining things Bob, does more for me than all the videos." Bill T., Ontario, Canada

"The cards arrived in sunny Australia safe and sound. Thanks very much. They are already speeding up my workflow!" Dave H. from Sydney, Australia

"Received the Tip Cards and decided to use pg.12 for extract. All one can say is "WOW" I was so impressed with that feature and the ease of use that I decided to change all the poor backgrounds in the Church Directory about (30 photos). It caused me more work but overall well worth the effort. Only 51 more cards to learn! Thanks again!" Tom Brayman, FL.

"Robert thanks so much for creating "Photoshop Tip Cards". I received them in the mail this afternoon, and have been trying them out all evening! The skin softening tip #41 (using filters) is fantastic. I took a photograph of myself and my husband from New Year's Eve and I think it made me look 10 years younger! I look forward to applying these recipes to more of my photos and taking my business to the next level. Sheryl T., Cloud Nine Photo Magic

"I had to learn the hard way. But I took lots of notes so you don't have to. They're all inside!"

Robert Schwarztrauber

PHOTOGRAPHY

Ezine @rticles

EXPERT AUTHOR

The Original Photoshop Tip Cards
"Don't <u>Learn</u> Photoshop...Just Do It!"

You don't have to go to culinary school
to cook a great meal.

You don't have train years as a carpenter's
apprentice to build great wood crafts.

You just need a few easy to follow plans.
Simple 'recipes' for success.

Now...You Have Them for Photoshop!

In this book are all the great Photoshop tips,
tricks and secret techniques used by the pros
to create stunning images fast!

Simple and Basic...designed for most Photoshop versions.

Over 100 tips in all!

**Plus... web site links
for even more
great skill building
and
profit making
opportunities!**

***Plus* Bonus...
Photographer's
Model Release Form!**

The Original
PHOTOSHOP TIP CARDS
by Robert M. Schwarztrauber

More **FREE** Tips and Info Can be Found at:

http://PhotoshopHouseofCards.blogspot.com
http://creativephotographytricks.com

The Photoshop Tip Card Story

They started as a few scribbles
on 3x5 index cards.
My desperate attempt to remember all the great
information I was finding while trying to
learn Photoshop.

Videos moved too fast. Websites I'd forget to
bookmark. Where's that darned DVD?

Eventually I made quite a collection of these 3x5
cards. I'd mention them in conversation and folks
would ask for copies. I started sharing them on my
blog—descriptions with more details.

Next came *"The Original Photoshop Tip Cards"*.
What started as a small fun project has evolved
into a big fun project.
I've gotten quite an education along the way.

I hope through this new book you can also get
great at Photoshop and come to enjoy your digital
photography more as well.

I want to personally thank you for your purchase.
I know these tips will help you too!

Beginners will catch on fast.
Pros might learn a few shortcuts
to speed up their workflow.

May all your photos become great ones!

Robert Schwarztrauber
PHOTOGRAPHY

Claim Your
Two **FREE** Bonus
PDF's Now!

Add great camera skills before you Photoshop and a way to sell your photos for cash after - and that's a winning combination!

Robert's Digital Photography Field Guide will help you capture the best photos in any situation. When you start with better photos, straight from the camera, your Photoshop editing process automatically becomesi so much easier! You can claim this PDF guide FREE with your purchase!

There is no better motivation than $$$. **101 Photo Ideas That Sell,** now in PDF form, lets you see just how to make money with your brand new Photoshop skills! Claim your FREE reports today by sending an email to the address below.

Send Your Request To: robert@photoshoptipcards.com

TABLE of CONTENTS

TABLE of CONTENTS

THE ORIGINAL PHOTOSHOP HOW-TO TIP CARDS

Let's Get

THE ORIGINAL PHOTOSHOP HOW-TO TIP CARDS

20 SINGLE KEY SHORTCUTS

Rather than use your mouse cursor to select a tool, simply touch the shortcut key shown here and that feature becomes active for use:

V = Move Tool

I = Eyedropper

L = Lasso Tool

Q = Quick Mask

D = Default Palette Colors (b/w)

M = Marquee Tool

C = Crop Tool

E = Eraser

B = Brushes

T = Text

H = Hand Tool

W = Magic Wand

J = Healing Brush

P = Pen Tool

S = Clone Stamp

Z = Zoom Tool

[= Change Tool Size (-)

] = Change Tool Size (+)

G = Paint Bucket

MORE KEYBOARD SHORTCUTS

- **Change OPACITY** quickly by pressing keypad numbers:

  Pressing #1 changes opacity to 10%, #2 to 20%, 3 to 30%, etc.
  Fast typers - get exact percentages by typing 2 numbers fast.

- **Change BLEND MODE:** press SHIFT (+) or SHIFT (-) to cycle through the options

- **Ctrl-R** turns the rulers on/off

- **Ctrl - SHIFT - U** for instant black & white images

- **Ctrl-C** to copy selection, then **Ctrl - V** to paste it elsewhere.

- **Esc** - press if you accidentally open a panel or activate a tool you did not want to use. The Esc key will cancel it. I use this most often if I want to cancel the crop tool.

3 STEPS TO GREAT PHOTOS

- **CROP** - Composition is key to producing great photographs. Be sure to fill the frame with your subject, crop to cut anything not needed to "tell the story". Keep in mind the "Rule of Thirds" when composing and cropping and also how "Diagonal Lines" lead your viewer's eye through the photo.

  It is always best to compose well using your camera, but cropping judiciously with Photoshop after, can often save the day.

- **LEVELS** - Whether you use **IMAGE-ADJUST-AUTO LEVELS** or the Manual version, **LAYER - NEW ADJUSTMENT LAYER -LEVELS** getting the exposure level correct is critical to great photographs

- **CURVES** - **LAYER - NEW ADJUSTMENT LAYER - CURVES** will add a nice "pop"/ definition to your work. Remember the "S" curve brings a bit of contrast to help create great photos.

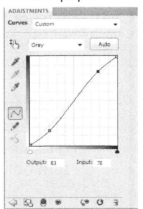

"If your photos aren't good enough, get closer."

Quote by Legendary Photographer
Robert Capa

Non-GLOBAL, Non-DESTRUCTIVE LAYER ADJUSTMENTS

When you want to use a layer adjustment, like LEVELS or CURVES or anything else under the LAYER > NEW ADJUSTMENT LAYER menu…

To effect only one layer and not the whole photo:

- **CTRL** click on the Layers thumbnail image to load it as a selection (you'll see the 'dancing ants' on your image)
- Go to **LAYER > NEW ADJUSTMENT LAYER** > (Your Choice)

A layer mask will automatically be created, hiding the adjustment areas outside of the selection.

You can also hold the ALT key and click between the adjustment layer and the one directly below to create a clipping mask so that only the layer below is changed.

QUICK TIPS

- This Plug-in Displays RAW files in Windows XP http://tinyurl.com/9k7aw

- Save for Web : **CTRL-SHIFT-ALT-S**

- Custom Brush Selection : with brush selected, hold **F5**

- Quickly change brush size with **[** key to smaller, **]** bigger

- **Ctrl - Alt - Shift - E** fills a blank layer with composite of below

- Shortcut **CTRL +** to zoom in, **CRTL -** to zoom out

- Fill Selection with foreground color : **Alt –Backspace**

- Fill Selection with background color: **Ctrl-Backspace**

- In new version CS-5, **SHIFT- F5** calls up content aware fill when a selection is active (marching ants)

THE ORIGINAL PHOTOSHOP HOW-TO TIP CARDS

MORE COOL TIPS

- **DRAW STRAIGHT LINES** - with your brush, size, and color selected, left click where you want to start your line, release, then move the curser to where your line should end, hold SHIFT and left click again and there's your straight line.

- **LAYER MASK -** When adding layer masks remember to paint with **opposite color to remove** the mask and **reveal** what's below (if mask is white, paint w/ black to remove mask) paint with same color as mask afterward to put the mask back. Lower the brush OPACITY to create more subtle changes

- **Ctrl - I** will INVERT or change your mask B/W qualities. If you have a black mask with white reveals, it will change to a white reveal with black masks,

BASIC PHOTO TUNE-UP

Exposure Levels

- **LAYER - NEW ADJUSTMENT LAYER - LEVELS**

- Slide Left (black level) arrow in toward right to meet first indication of black on histogram.

- Slide Right (white level) arrow in toward left to meet first white indication on Histogram

Contrast

- **LAYER - NEW ADJUSTMENT LAYER - CURVES**

  At top right of first box (lower left) drag line **down** a very little at a 45 degree angle.

  At bottom left of top right box, drag line up a very little. It should look like an "S'" curve when done. This will improve your contrast greatly.

PINPOINT ACCURACY with LEVELS ADJUSTMENT

The levels adjustment is one of the most used adjustments. Most often, the sliders are just moved in and out until it "looks good". There is however, a way to gauge the optimal position.

- **LAYER - NEW ADJUSTMENT LAYER - LEVELS**

- Hold down the **ALT** key as you move the slider.

-

- Your image will turn white as you move the right (dark) slider toward the center. The image returns just as the lightest pixels begins to darken. Stop there.

- As you move the left (light) slider, your image will go black and then reappear just as the darkest pixel begins to lighten. Stop there.

- Using this method you'll have no inadvertent clipping (loss of pixels)!

CLARITY PERCENTAGES

- Often times, as we're going thru our workflow, the image seems to appear not sharp. Edges are jagged.

- In order to speed screen size changes as we zoom in and out through the range of enlargements and reductions we use as we work on our images, Photoshop only recalculates certain percentages accurately. On all the others it just "roughs it" leading to seemingly lower resolution image properties.

- Accurate percentage values are 12.5%, 25%, 50% & 100%

When doing fine, detailed (especially edge) adjustments, make sure you are working at one of those 4 accurate zoom percentages when viewing on your screen.

THE 4 MOST USEFUL BLEND MODES

- **MULTIPLY -** Darkens the darkest pixels, while having no effect on the lightest. Great for fixing an overexposed photograph quickly.

- **SCREEN -** Lightens the lightest pixels while ignoring the darkest. Great for lightening underexposed photos and lightening photos prior to printing. Most monitors, unless calibrated, make the photo appear lighter than it is, so then when it prints it looks too dark.

  Duplicate finished photo, change layer to SCREEN mode, then reduce opacity to between 20% to 55% prior to printing.

- **OVERLAY -** Multiplies Effects, great for quick color enhancement. On a properly exposed photo, use Ctrl-J to duplicate layer, change blend mode to Overlay, then reduce OPACITY for a great look.

- **SOFTLIGHT -** Similar to Overlay, but Creates a softer, more even appearance across the image.

STRAIGHTEN HORIZON

- Right click on the **EYEDROPPER** to reveal **MEASURE TOOL** (It looks like a little ruler)

- With measure tool selected, left mouse click on one end of an element that you know should be horizontal, then, using the mouse, drag a line to the right side of that same line.

- Release mouse. (don't worry, the line doesn't actually draw on your photo)

- Go to **IMAGE - ROTATE CANVAS - ARBITRARY,** click **OK**

- The entire photo is then automatically repositioned to perfect horizontal.

- Adjust as needed to please the eye.

- CROP the image to correct for any edge defects.

BETTER EXTRACTIONS

Great tip for when you want to extract a tricky subject - like something with hair or fur!

SELECT - make a rough selection around the object you wish to cut out

CLICK **REFINE EDGE** in the top toolbar

1. Check the box 'Smart Radius'

2. Slide the Radius Slide to fine tune the edges to include more.

3. Select the refine edge brush and trace all around your subject with the brush.

Use adjust edge tools like slide edge to fine tune and then check decontaminate colors (in background, if needed) then output as desired (I use new layer w/ mask)

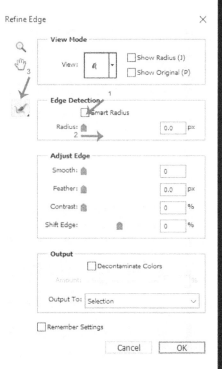

UNIVERSAL CONTRAST CORRECTION

(quick adjustment using auto features)

- **Ctrl-J** to duplicate your original

- **Image - Adjustments - Auto Levels**

- **Ctrl-J** to duplicate this new adjusted layer

- **Image - Adjustments - Equalize**

- Change **BLEND MODE** to **SOFTLIGHT and drop OPACITY to between 30% - 50%**

- **LAYER - MERGE VISIBLE**

QUICK HIGH-KEY IMAGES

- With your background layer selected
  IMAGE - MODE - CMYK

- **Move to the CHANNELS tab behind
  LAYERS,** (click WINDOWS-CHANNELS if
  you don't see the channels tab and check
  'channels')

- **select BLACK**

- Use keyboard shortcuts:
  Ctrl-A to select the whole image
  and see "marching ants"
  Ctrl-C to copy to clipboard
- Activate (click on) top CMYK layer, press
  Ctrl-V to paste

Going back to your LAYERS, you can
reduce the opacity of this layer to bring
more color back, or add a mask and paint
areas (lips, eyes etc.) back in selectively

RESIZE without CROP or DISTORTION

- Go to **IMAGE - IMAGE SIZE**

- Uncheck - Constrain Proportion

- Check - Resample Bicubic

- Change/Input desired Width/Height , example, 5x7 or 8x10

Note: to maintain overall pixel clarity when enlarging it is best to go up in small increments. Going directly from 4x6 to 16x20 will create loss of quality as program 'makes up' or 'creates' too many pixels to complete the task well.

SUPER FAST SELECTIONS
Using Color Range

If your image has a large area of similar color that you want to select without using the selection tools like the lasso or magic wand, try this:

- Go to **SELECT > COLOR RANGE**
  You get a dialog box and an eyedropper to sample the color you want to select

- Click the **EYEDROPPER** on the color you want to select

- Move the fuzziness slider until that area of color shows completely white on your dialog box.

- Click **OK** and the "ants" will begin to dance, letting you know you have made your selection.

- >>> **Bonus Tip!** Clicking **INVERT** will switch your selection. Often makes removing subjects from solid backgrounds very easy.

Example: Select the blue sky around your subject, then invert to take your subject out of the picture and paste into a new scene.

COLOR CHANGES WITH
HUE / SATURATION

For deeper more intense colors:

- **Layer - New Layer Adjustment - Hue/ Saturation**

- To intensify color throughout, use the MASTER default edit and slide the saturation to the right.

- To intensify ONE particular color and leave the rest unchanged, change the MASTER edit to the color (or family of colors you want to change instead.

- Desaturate by sliding left

- Create black & white photos by taking the slider full to the left.

WHITE BALANCE
using LEVELS

- **LAYER - NEW ADJUSTMENT LAYER - LEVELS** 3 eyedroppers will appear as color samplers.

- Use the center eyedropper to set the white balance by clicking in your photo on a neutral color. Metal objects work well or object that appear 50% gray. Click around until you feel the white balance is correct.

- Sample with the left most eyedropper to set the black level, click on something black in the image.

- Sample with the right most eyedropper to set the white level by clicking in the image on something that you know should be white.

- Use the sliders on the histogram to fine tune your white balance.

INSTANT 'POP'

A quick and easy way to add more intense color and sharpness. It's the color/contrast "wow" you never knew you needed!

- Duplicate your background layer **[ctrl-J]**

- Change Blend mode to:
  Soft Light - for a little "pop"
  Overlay - for intense "pop"

- Adjust the **OPACITY** then to lesson the "pop" until it's just perfect for you

PRINTS
TURN OUT TOO DARK

On your finished photo, after all adjustments have been made,

- Flatten Layers, then Press **[crtl-j]** to duplicate (this reduces final file size) or

- Create a new combined layer at the top by pressing **[ctrl-alt-shift-e]**

- Change **BLEND MODE** on this new layer to **SCREEN**. You should immediately see photo go too light.

- Reduce **OPACITY** to between **25% - 55%** depending on the qualities of your photo and final print preference.

I typically save the file then with some indication it is a print file, sometime I end the file name with P or sometimes J.

Printing too dark happens because our monitors are often too bright and give a false representation. You can buy a buy a monitor calibration tool, (expensive) but this technique has always worked very well for me.

GLOW

This technique puts a nice soft glow effect on images. Works very well on portraits.

- Duplicate the Background (Ctrl-J)

- **Filter - Blur - Gaussian Blur** (8-25 pixels)

- Adjust Radius - Blurs All

- Change Blend Mode on that layer to Soft Light
    Layer - **Soft light**
    Adjust the **Opacity** slider to change the intensity of the effect

- Spot - Effects - Blending option slider this layer for Start/Stop of blur

- Hold down **Alt** to split the triangle for a smoother transition - no posterizing

QUICK FIX
for OVEREXPOSER
& UNDEREXPOSER

In both cases, the first step is to duplicate your image

- Keyboard shortcut, **Ctrl-J**

If overexposed, (image is too light)
- Change the **BLEND MODE** on your new layer to **MULTIPLY**

If underexposed, (image is too dark)
- Change the **BLEND MODE** on your new layer to **SCREEN**

- Decrease the **OPACITY** to fine tune the effects.

CHANGING THE GRID

Using **VIEW > SHOW GRID** can make composing our images much easier. But the default grid is not always the best choice.

To easily change it:

- Go to **EDIT > PREFERENCES > GUIDES, GRIDS and SLICES**

- In the dialog box, under **GRIDLINE EVERY** enter a value of **33.3** and change the measure box to **PERCENT**

- Next, change the **Subdivisions** to **2**

This will divide your surface nicely into 9 boxes which are great for composition because they simulate the Rule of Thirds.

Feel free to set any preference you need depending on the type of work you do.

HISTORY EXTENSION
(need more UNDO's?)

- **EDIT - PREFERENCES - GENERAL or (PERFORMANCE) - HISTORY STATES**

- Change the default (20) to a higher number

A word of caution! HISTORY consumes HUGE memory. The higher you make this value, the slower your processing becomes. (best kept under 50)

Or, if you have a lot of pics to process that could get by with maybe one or two undo commands, lower the history setting to speed up your work.

WARM IT UP
- COOL IT DOWN

Dramatically change the feel of your image by adding a color tone layer on top

- Add a new, blank layer (we're going to fill it with color)

- Click on the foreground color pallet to change the R, G, B settings

- To warm it up, start with red 235, green 177 and blue 19.

- To cool down the photo, try red 0, green 34 and blue 205.

- Using the **PAINT BUCKET**, click layer to dump the paint color on

- Set the **BLEND MODE** to **COLOR** with **OPACITY** 15-25%

Experiment with the colors to get just the look you need

ANTIQUE LOOK

- **IMAGE - ADJUST - DESATURATE**

- **IMAGE - ADJUST - COLOR BALANCE**
  Move bottom slider toward yellow (old sepia like tones)

- **FILTER - ARTISTIC - FILM GRAIN**
  Adjust 3 sliders for desired effect,
  as a guide / good starting point:

  Grain **3**
  Highlight **1**
  Intensity **1**

CREATE 'OLD STYLE' PHOTO EFFECT

- **Ctrl - J** to duplicate Background
- **Ctrl - Shift - U** to turn into Black & White
- **Ctrl - J** to duplicate B/W Rename "COLOR"
- **Ctrl - J** to duplicate again Rename "NOISE"
- On "COLOR" layer, choose army green or sepia tone foreground color, Alt-Backspace to fill over layer. Reduce Opacity to 20%
- On "NOISE" layer, **FILTER - NOISE - ADD NOISE** (ex.30%)
- Choose Distribution:Uniform,
- Choose **MONOCHROMATIC**

Reduce noise opacity (to ~45%)

- Use eraser tool to reveal important features like face
- Darken Edges using non-destructive dodge/burn

PHOTO TO PENCIL STYLE
(best with not too much detailed textures)

- Duplicate Background

- Set foreground color to black

- **FILTER - OTHER - HIGH PASS** (set radius very small - photo will now look gray)

- **FILTER - SKETCH - NOTE PAPER**
  Set Image Balance: 25
  Graininess: 0
  Relief: 0
  (OK)

- IMAGE - ADJUST - **THRESHOLD**
  Adjust slider to right to make the lines more black (OK)

You can also reduce the OPACITY to create some cool colored art!

PHOTOS TO
PENCIL SKETCHES
For Portraits

- Duplicate Background **LAYER - NEW - LAYER VIA COPY**

- Desaturate Layer 1 **IMAGE - ADJUST - DESATURATE**

- Duplicate Layer 1 **LAYER - NEW - LAYER VIA COPY**

- On Layer 2, **IMAGE - ADJUST - INVERT** (looks like negative now)

- Change Blend Mode on Layer 2 to Color Dodge (now looks white)

- **FILTER - BLUR - GAUSSIAN BLUR** Move slider full left, then creep up right until it looks good

Try also with motion blur and radial blur.

CENTER YOUR IMAGE

To center your image on the canvas…

- Select the layer or layers you would like to center (Hold down the **CTRL** key to select more than one layer)

- On the toolbar **SELECT > ALL**, you'll see the "dancing ants" appear

- Select the **MOVE** tool and several alignment options will appear on the toolbar above, combinations of verticals and horizontals.

- With your mouse, click on the one(s) that you need and Photoshop will move Your selected layer(s) to that position within the canvas dimension, no need to guess where perfectly centered is.

Works for any layer type, image or text

ADD WHITE BORDER
TO PHOTOS

- **Ctrl-J** to duplicate your layer

- Press '**D**' to set color pallet to default black/white

- Go to **IMAGE - CANVAS SIZE** - (once here change your measuring scale from inches to pixels for both the height and width

- **add 50 to 100 pixels** equally to what-ever height and width values are shown (your preference on how much border you'd like to have) Click, 'OK" and you're done.

Tip: If it turns out your border is black, it's OK! Just grab a bucket of white paint and dump it on the border to change the color...it's easy to forget to change the color palette first.

CREATE A QUICK FRAME

- **LAYER - NEW - LAYER**

- Move to top position

- Select **COLOR** for your border

- Click **PAINT BUCKET** onto image to make border color layer

- Reduce opacity to view picture beneath

- Click **VIEW** to turn on RULERS and SNAP (check the boxes to turn on)

- Click POINT (move) TOOL to drag line from side/top onto picture. Space all 4 sides evenly using ruler guides.

-
- Use the MARQUEE tool to mark off centered rectangle area (the ants dance)

- **LAYER - NEW - LAYER via CUT**

- Turn off EYEBALL leaving only border, then readjust OPACITY

FOOL-PROOF BORDER FRAMES...3D GRADIENT

(This example uses a typical 4x6 photo layout, but technique works for any size)

Once you have your photo adjusted and ready to print:

- **IMAGE - CANVAS SIZE** - add one inch to width & height (5x7)
- Using eyedropper tool, select a color for your border from your photo
- Add **LAYER** - Use Marquee tool around entire new photo size
- Use **PAINT BUCKET** to cover **MARQUEE** area w/ chosen color
- **SELECT - MODIFY - BORDER,** set at 200 pixels
- **SELECT - INVERSE**, use delete on keyboard to reveal photo

(Optional: choose another color or the same and PAINT BUCKET inside frame again)

Because you select the colors from your photo, they always coordinate well!

SOFTEN
An Alternative to Gaussian Blur

- **Filter > Noise > Median**

- With Preview Mode turned on (check the box) gradually move slider to the right to soften (blur) your subject

Not so great for overall (whole images) but works great when you have a particular subject on it's own layer that you would like to soften, because Median will blur (soften) the inside but leave the edges sharp.

Try this for softer skin.

UNDERSTANDING
THE UNSHARP MASK

FILTER - SHARPEN - UNSHARP MASK

- **AMOUNT** - controls the sharpening intensity (1%-500%) by making the lighter pixels lighter/the dark darker. Maximum changes at 500%. It's responsible for the white "halo" on edges.(For best results, keep the value between 50-150%) Lower Values reduce halo effect.

- **RADIUS** - controls width of the sharpening halo (.1%-250%) Or how many edge pixels it checks and changes. Best to change this setting first (best kept under (4) and reduce AMOUNT as you go up on AMOUNT.

- **THRESHOLD** - sets how different neighboring pixels have to be before PS considers them an edge. (0-255). At 0 all the pixels on image will be sharpened. (best range is between 3 - 20)

Tip: My standard setting for every use is:
AMOUNT= 50%
RADIUS= 1.1 pixel
THRESHOLD = 1

TEXT AS SHAPE

- Create a **TEXT** layer and be certain to triple check your spelling and be sure this is the type font you wish to use. After the next step you won't be able to change this, although you are always free to start over.

- **LAYER - TYPE - CONVERT TO SHAPE**

  Now you're free to reshape text, turn it into perspective view or whatever. But you cannot change the individual letters after you convert. Here's how to customize text:

- **EDIT – FREE TRANSFORM**
  Use to reposition or reshape your complete text shape. You can also use the TRANSFORM feature to reshape, or flip the text too. Nice for creating a reflection or shadow effect.

FLATTEN
without FLATTENING

- **LAYER - FLATTEN IMAGE** is most often used to condense all the adjustment layers and preview your final image before saving and printing.

  But, except for the undo commands (EDIT - UNDO or EDIT– STEP BACKWARD) You could no longer make changes to layers. This limits our options.

- Instead, add a new layer to the top level, then press:

- **Ctrl - Alt - SHIFT - E**   All the active layers below will be merged and placed in this top level. Same as flattening, but you can still view your adjustment layers and make changes.

  If you need to make changes to layers below, delete this composite layer and recreate after you've made needed changes.

ULTRA SHARP EYES

Basically we'll lighten the colored portion of the eyes and darken the pupil and the outer colored edge of the iris.

- Duplicate your background layer

- Select the **DODGE** tool, small size to lighten the iris

  Set at **MIDTONES**, exposure less than 20%

- Select the **BURN** tool, small size and soft to darken the outer edge of iris and the pupil. Small size, set at **SHADOW** Exposure less than 15%

You can also use the non-destructive dodge and burn techniques seen earlier in this book. (I usually do).

Remember:

DODGE = LIGHTEN

BURN = DARKEN

EYE COLOR - ENHANCE OR CHANGE

- Duplicate your background layer

- Use the **Elliptical Marquee** tool to rough outline the iris

- Select **Quick Mask** (w/color indicates masked area)

- Use **brush tool** w /hard edge to paint mask up to iris edge (zoom in tight for best accuracy)

-
- Return to **Standard Mode** (click box to left of Quick Mask)

- **LAYER - NEW - LAYER**
  then **EDIT - FILL** with your color choice

- Choose a blend mode (hue, overlay, softlight, multiply) that works well for you and adjust the opacity to your needs

- Duplicate the eye layer and use move tool to place over second eye. Erase excess or use healing brush to add

EYES THAT SPARKLE

- Duplicate your background
- Hold Alt while adding new layer from layers palette
   In dialog box, choose OVERLAY, Fill with 50% gray (you should see a gray layer appear at top position)
- Use dodge tool on HIGHLIGHT to lighten catchlights a bit
- Use dodge tool on MIDTONES to lighten whites a bit
- Use dodge tool - MIDTONES to lighten between pupil & iris edge
- Merge down layers
- Use Crtl-J to create a SHARPENING Layer, then on this new, duplicated layer:
- FILTER - SHARPEN - UNSHARP MASK T:4, R:3.5 A: 150
- Add BLACK mask to layer to keep from sharpening skin and background. Paint then with WHITE over iris, lashes to sharpen only. Use a low opacity, soft-edge brush to build to best level.

SKIN SOFTEN with HIGH PASS FILTER

- Duplicate your background layer

- Change **Blend Mode** to **Overlay**

- **FILTER - OTHER - HIGH PASS**
  Set pixels value to 9.5 and click OK
  (photo gets blurry)

- Press **Ctrl-I** to invert the layer and begin reducing the **Opacity** until a nice smoothness is achieved overall, but not overdone to look fake/plastic

- Add a Layer Mask and paint over to return sharpness to features (eyes, lips eyebrows, hair, etc.)

REMOVE DARK CIRCLES
UNDER EYES

- Duplicate your background layer

- Select the **HEALING BRUSH**
  Choose an appropriate size brush with a feathered edge, Select a very low hardness (around 5%)

- Change the default mode from **NORMAL** to **REPLACE**

- Sample a nearby area to eye bags & stroke smoothly over the dark areas

- For a more subtle effect, lower the opacity of that layer when finished with the healing brush.

SELECTIVE SHARPENING

This technique allows you to sharpen only parts of an image. Often used in portraits to keep skin soft but make the eyes tack sharp.

- Duplicate Layer (ctrl-J)

- Use **Filter - Other - High Pass**

- Set Radius (10-30 pixels)

- Change Layer Blend Mode to **Softlight** or **Overlay**

- Add Layer Mask while holding down Alt (mask should show black)

- Brush desired area with a **white brush** to selectively sharpen only that area. (Use a soft or hard edged brush depending on the effect you desire)

ISOLATE ONE LAYER

If you want to work on just one layer, without all the distraction of the others, here's how to turn off all the other layers with just three clicks. This technique works well if you find there is some unwanted element in your image but you can't figure out which layer it is coming from.

- Select (click on) the layer you wish to keep visible

- Right Click on that layers "eyeball" on the far left

- Select **SHOW/HIDE all other layers**

When you're finished, simply reverse the process and all the other layers turn back on together too.

TURN SCOWLS INTO SMILES

- Duplicate your background layer

- **FILTER - LIQUIFY**

    - Select the Warp Tool (finger tool at the top left)
    - Set the Brush Size about the size of the mouth
    - Set the Brush Pressure 50-70
    - Click just outside each mouth corner and gentle drag UP until a slight smile appears. Too much will look fake.

You can also use the EDIT - PUPPET WARP tool but it is a bit more complex.

SELECTIVE COLOR
to ENHANCE CONTRAST

- **LAYER - NEW ADJUSTMENT LAYER - SELECTIVE COLOR**

- Select "NEUTRALS" from the COLORS drop-down. Move the BLACK slider to improve the look

- Repeat with "BLACK" and "WHITE" choices in the drop down

Once your Neutrals, Blacks and Whites are done to improve Contrast, you can also tweak your other colors to improve the balance by selecting them from the drop-down and moving their color matched sliders

ADD 'POP'
with GAUSSIAN BLUR

- **Ctrl-J** to duplicate your image on the layers pallet

- **FILTER—BLUR - GAUSSIAN BLUR** (adjust slider until you can just see shapes well, but the rest is blurred)

- Change **BLEND MODE to OVERLAY Or SOFTLIGHT**

Experiment!

Instead of **OVERLAY** try **VIVID** or **HARD LIGHT** and/or vary the **OPACITY** to get the look that's best for you.

SIMPLIFIED Non-Destructive DODGE and BURN

A simple, adjustable, non-permanent way to selectively lighten or darken parts of your image.

- Create a new blank Layer

- Change **BLEND MODE** to **SOFTLIGHT**

- Using a soft round **BRUSH** tool, set at opacity 5-20%, paint with WHITE to lighten selected areas, paint with BLACK to darken areas

- If you make a mistake, use eraser tool over that area and try again.

- You can use **[ctrl-e]** to merge this layer permanently with your original once complete or leave as a stand-alone layer in case you wish to make additional changes later.

REMOVE
CREASES AND WRINKLES

Creases
Whenever your subjects head is turned, it's likely you'll find some creases in the neck. Use the **Spot Healing** or **Healing Brush** tools on a new layer, set to **Sample All Layers**. Click little by little along the creases rather than trying to remove them in one sweep. If you get close to the edges of the neck, switch to the **Clone Stamp** tool to prevent the healing brushes dragging in areas outside the skin, which will result in a discolored area.

Wrinkles
Use the same technique to remove forehead wrinkles and wrinkles in the cheeks. Wrinkles around the eyes are best removed by moving in close with the **Clone Stamp** tool because of the proximity of the eye and lashes. To maintain some realism, lower the opacity of your new layer to prevent things from looking too smooth.

If your are super serious about learning how to retouch skin and create portraits like the pros, search Youtube for videos on **Frequency Separation**. It takes some practice to get the hang of, but once you do there is no better way to create realistic, professional quality portraits.

SHARPEN
WITH HIGH PASS FILTER

- Open Image, duplicate background using (**Ctrl-J**)

- Set **BLEND** mode to **OVERLAY**

- **FILTER - OTHER - HIGH PASS**

- Drag slider until all colors just disappear (<10 pixels?) **OK**

- Slide **OPACITY** down to zero then back up to look for best amount of sharpening effect.

FASTER CUT-OUTS

Use the Magic Wand tool on the area that has the most consistent color/texture. Many times, this is not the subject we wish to cut out but rather the background.

After using the magic wand to select our background area rather than our subject:

- **SELECT - INVERSE**.
  Now instead of the background being selected, your subject is. You can lift your subject out now by choosing:

- **LAYER - NEW - LAYER VIA COPY** (or CUT if you prefer)

Tip: Holding **SHIFT** with Magic Wand lets you select (add) multiple areas at one time. Each mouse click adds to the last so you can incorporate many colors and background texture to form one unit for extraction purposes.

CUT and PASTE
EDGE CURE –DEFRINGE

Sometimes when you cut a subject out to paste elsewhere you find that the edges also contain little bits of background from the image you took your subject from.

A Quick Fix for that is while your subject cut-out layer is active,

LAYER - MATTING - DEFRINGE

Select how many of the outer edge pixels should be removed to clean up the edges. (2 pixels should be minimum)

You can run this continuously until the edges become clean.

Use a Gaussian blur or soft eraser to further smooth if needed and if useful for your application.

PERSPECTIVE CORRECTION

(aka. Keystone Effect, leaning vertical lines)

- Correct for **STRAIGHTEN HORIZON** as your first step

- Duplicate Layer (to use keyboard short-cut, press Ctrl-J)

- **VIEW - SHOW - GRID** (turns ON grid reference lines)

- **EDIT - FREE TRANSFORM**

- Drag corners holding **CTRL** until the best vertical lines align w/grid

- Drag center/top straight up to regain normal height perspective.

- Press **ENTER** to lock in changes

- **CROP** sides to eliminate run-off

- **VIEW - SHOW - GRID** (to now turn OFF grid lines)

SLIDING SUBJECTS
into CONTAINERS

This is a neat trick to make it look like your subject is inside a bowl, a barrel, a cup, a box or anything!

- Press **Ctrl-J** to duplicate background
- On the new layer use the **LASSO** tool to trace around the outer edge of your (The 'ants' start marching)
- **LAYER - NEW - LAYER via COPY**
- Cut subject from separate photo, clean edges then DRAG or COPY into your container picture
- Position the subject layer BETWEEN the original background and the cutout layer.
- Adjust color and lighting so subject and background match

Note: especially watch that the lighting/ shadow sides are consistent. For realism, light can't appear to come strongly from two directions at once.

DROP SHADOW SHORTCUT

An easy way to position shadow on your text layers.

- On your TEXT layer, right mouse click to **BLENDING OPTIONS**

- Choose **DROP SHADOW**, OK

- Double Click on **the DROP SHADOW** effects layer to open adjustments

- Instead of using the **DISTANCE & ANGLE** settings, simply go on to your image, hold down the left mouse button and drag your shadow to wherever you'd like it to be!

SIMPLE SHADOWS
FROM BRUSHES

When you need to put a shadow behind something, maybe a subject you've cutout and dragged in, anything on a transparent background:

- Select the BRUSH tool

- Duplicate the layer you wish to shadow,

- On the tool bar above, next to the brush sizes, change the MODE to "**Behind**" instead of the default of Normal

- Adjust your brush size and opacity as desired. A soft brush usually works best for shadows.

- Paint the shadow in wherever you'd like it. In this mode the brush tool won't paint over any opaque (colored) pixels so your artwork is protected.

ADD A SHADOW

- Duplicate Layer (ctrl-J)

- Select Subject with choice of Magic Wand, Lasso, Marquee tool, or pen tool

- **LAYER - NEW - LAYER via COPY** rename this layer SUBJECT

- Create a new layer, reselect your subject, then with the **PAINT BUCKET** tool, choose color **BLACK**, and click inside the 'marching ants' on your newly created layer. Call this layer SHADOW

- Move SHADOW layer below SUBJECT layer, like sandwich Subject, Shadow, Original Layer

- **FILTER - BLUR - GAUSSIAN BLUR** to 9.3, opacity 54 (or adjust as needed)

- Use arrow to move (offset) shadow behind subject however you like

- Use **EDIT - FREE TRANSFORM to customize shadow** for additional realism

MERGE SHADOW or
2 OR MORE OBJECTS

These two keyboard shortcuts are useful when you need to combine multiple layers, something which can be very important because if you need to move things around later, you need all the elements to move together.

- **LAYER - MERGE DOWN or CTRL-E**
  For example, use this if you have created a shadow by duplicating your subject and you want to be sure the two will move together if need be.

- Alternately, you may want to use one of the most useful keyboard shortcuts, **Ctrl - ALT - SHIFT - E** which will add a new layer on top which is a composite of all the visible layers below it.

SHALLOW DEPTH OF FIELD

(blurred background or foreground)

- Duplicate Background Layer **(Ctrl– J)** (rename that layer 'Background Blur')

- Use the **Lasso** tool (outline subject, not exact, get marching ants

- Set Feather Amount (80 is good)

- **LAYER - NEW - LAYER via COPY** (Layer 1 =subject)

- On Background Blur layer, use **FILTER - GAUSSIAN BLUR**

- Adjust to Correct Blur Level (10-80)

- Optional, Adjust Opacity to 60-80%

- Use Eraser on Background Blur to un-blur areas that need it.

- **LAYER - FLATTEN IMAGE**

USING "CLONE"
as COPY TOOL

(A great technique when poor expressions or other annoyances appear in photos – this adds a cloned layer overlay to fix those bad photos)

- Open the two similar photos in Photoshop, select the **CLONE** tool

- On the "good" image, **Alt-Left-Mouse** Click anywhere in the photo to clone (copy) the entire image

- On your other photo, **Ctrl-J** to copy, then add new LAYER

- With new, blank layer active, hold down left-mouse button and "paint" your cloned layer onto this new layer

The beauty is you can "paint" as little or as much as you like!   Eliminate blinking, frowns, hair out of place etc.

STARBURST EFFECTS

(works best when there are several random bright spots in or placed in your image)

- Duplicate your background, 2 times (now have 3 layers) [ctrl-J, ctrl-J]

- Top Layer, **FILTER - BLUR - MOTION BLUR** Change angle to **45*** maximum distance: 999

- Now turn off this layer (hide) top layer

- Middle Layer, **FILTER - BLUR - MOTION BLUR** Change angle to **- 45*** maximum distance: 999

- Return to top layer, change blend mode to screen and then **IMAGE-MERGE DOWN**

- Change the Blend mode on this new combined layer to screen

- **Layer-New Adjustment Layer– Levels** to re-darken. You can fine tune this layer using a 10% opacity eraser or a layer mask

BEND WITH SHEAR FILTER

- **Duplicate** your background layer

- Enlarge Canvas, **IMAGE - CANVAS SIZE**, double W & H

- Shear filter only bends a vertical object left or right, so you may need to change the orientation of your image first. Use: **EDIT- TRANSFORM - 90*cw or ccw**

- **FILTER - DISTORT - SHEAR**
  In grid box, click and hold as you move the center, solid vertical line right or left to bend your photo (much like the "curves" adjustment). Click **"OK"** when you're finished

- Rotate back if needed, then crop to finished size or cut out bent object for use elsewhere.

DRAW PERFECTLY
STRAIGHT LINES
with TOOLS

Draw Straight Lines with Brushes

- Choose your brush size, for line we Usually use a hard-edged brush, small.

- Click on your starting point, then hold the Shift key, and click again where you want the line to end. Photoshop will draw a straight line between the two points. To create angular shapes, just keep clicking around.

- Also works with most other tools, including erasers and even the highlight tool in the Extract filter.

Tip: If you are painting using a layer mask, holding down the shift key, creating lines in short segments, even around curves, will produce a less pixilated outcome than if you were just dragging the curser around the object.

SPECIAL CHARACTER TIPS

Sometimes we need to add symbols to indicate that a property (text or image) is owned or sourced from another.

Here's how to add (C) copyright, (R) registered, or (TM) trademark logo in Photoshop:

• Create a new text layer

• Hold down the **alt** key and use the
• **numbers pad** of your keyboard:

copyright - (alt) 0169 = ©
registered - (alt) 0174 = ®
trademark - (alt) 0153 = ™

When you release the **alt** key, the symbol will appear.

COLOR PALETTE QUICK TIPS
Quickly Changing Brush Colors

The default colors on the palette swatches are BLACK and WHITE. But we often change them in our work process.

A super quick way to reset them from our chosen colors back to black and white is to use keyboard shortcuts.

Press letter **D**
Will reset the color swatches to Black and White

Press letter **X**
To toggle between current foreground and background colors

THE END

**But with photography tips,
It's never the end!**

READ ON

**for more great
Photography Resources**

MORE...

FREE PHOTOGRAPHY
TIPS and TRICKS

**Improve your skills and
amaze your friends
using *even more* simple,
yet little known tips
from my unique photography
websites:**

CreativePhotographyTricks.com

PhotoshopHouseOfCards.blogspot.com

RobertsPhotoNews.com

Create Your Own Photoshop Recipes!

Print This Page To Jot Down Your Best PS Tips!

Photographic Release

For valuable consideration received, I hereby grant to

_____ (Photographer)

and his/her legal representatives and assigns, the irrevocable and unrestricted right to use and publish photographs of me, or in which I may be included, for editorial, trade, advertising, and any other purpose and in any manner and medium; to alter the same without restriction; and to copyright the same. I hereby release Photographer and his/her legal representatives and assigns from all claims and liability relating to said photographs.

Date _____

Name _____

Address _____

_____

Signature _____

If minor. signature _____
of guardian

Witness _____

Based upon sample release from the American Society of Media Photographers. You **must** consult your lawyer to determine validity before usage.

Made in the USA
Monee, IL
19 January 2021

58076490R00049